JUST
MUSHROOMS
celebrating the future of food

Dedicated to the person holding this book;
thank you for supporting our delicious vision
of a more sustainable tomorrow.

JUST
MUSHROOMS

celebrating the future of food

FOREWORD BY
MICHAEL MYHRE, MD.

MICHELLE RUSSELL

+

CAMILLE DEGABRIELLE

INTERIOR DESIGN BY
LILIANA GUIA

COVER DESIGN BY
CAMILLE DEGABRIELLE

RECIPE PHOTOGRAPHY BY
JEFF MENSCH

CONTENTS

sides + snacks

desserts

wellness

appendix

index

bibliography

foreword

Just Mushrooms is an appropriately simple title for a book intended to be a tasty introduction to the culinary delights of the world of mushrooms. This book, in which the central ingredient in all recipes is some form of readily available mushroom, was written to provide pragmatic culinary direction to newcomers and experienced mycophiles alike.

This is a world to which I was a newcomer until recently; I am the guy when my daughter and son-in-law brought home pounds of freshly foraged wild mushrooms from the nearby mountains, I greeted their foraging success as a dangerously foolhardy enterprise sure to result in an ER visit, or worse.

It didn't, and the mushrooms they found were delicious. Nobody died, nobody even got sick.

You see, for the three or more prior decades I worked as a pathologist, and while I had encountered fungi in college as a fascinating member of a biological kingdom, I have since only known those fungi that often do great harm to people. I knew only the harm fungi can do to people, having built a medical reference laboratory whose prime goal was immediate accurate diagnosis of pretty much everything, including disseminated fungal infections.

This changed when I joined my son-in-law Ketchum at a weekend course on mycology and mushrooms taught by Peter McCoy, his Radical Mycology course. At that course I learned that the mycological world is perhaps the single greatest unexplored territory in biological science. As opposed to those to which I was accustomed to studying these fungi hold great potential not only as nourishment, but also as a means of improving peoples' health, sometimes dramatically – but they hold the keys to detoxifying, recycling and feeding the world.

This was brought home to me in a dramatic fashion when my wife Gloria tested positive for West Nile virus after donating blood. Gloria, ordinarily an impressive bundle of irrepressible energy, began suffering nightly headaches and a sort of malaise she attributed to the vagaries of aging. At my son-in-law's suggestion, she tried turkey tail tea, a traditional remedy for viral illnesses.

Much to my surprise, with the very first cup of turkey tail tea Gloria's headache and malaise faded away on the spot. To this day, she swears by turkey tail tea, the recipe for which you will find in this book (*page 73*).

I had to know more. I started buying books on fungi, found myself reading and collecting mycology textbooks, I signed up for a mycology course at Boise State University and joined the mycology association. I even built my own little mycology laboratory so I could grow and study these remarkable creatures myself. I have become a full blown mycophile, someone who seemingly sees a connection to the fungal world in everything.

This is because fungi are everywhere; invisible to our naked eyes, we live in clouds of trillions of fungal spores which cumulatively represent perhaps the largest biomass on our planet. If aliens landed on Earth and surveyed for living entities, they could be forgiven if they thought that this planet was ruled by fungi. At some level, it is: the fungal component of lichens break down mountain rocks into soil to deliver nutrients to plants that make this planet habitable, and ultimately feed us all. It is fungi that inhabit the cells of plant roots, living inside the cells of vast majority of plants. Quite simply, plants could not survive without fungi, and we could not survive without plants.

It was fungi that roughly 300 million years ago developed the ability to decompose cellulose an lignin, ending the deposition of the world's carbon deposits destined to become petrochemicals and beginning the recycling of detritus into component parts usable by new living organisms. They are the central hub of ecology; fungi provide the building blocks of life. They live in the air around us, their spores seed rain clouds to initiate rainstorms; they live beneath us in the soil, miles of mycelial threads course through every square inch of soil beneath our feet. They live on us, in us, fungi are our unseen helpers, everywhere.

They are also the ultimate survivors; their spores can survive exposure to cosmic rays and even the complete vacuum of deep space. Fungi destined for an experiment even survived the explosion of a spacecraft en route to the International Space Station.

As luck would have it, mushrooms are among the most delicious and nutritious foods on the planet. One that can be raised economically and in ways better for the health of the planet in the process.

When I met Michelle Russell at a farmers market in Boise a couple of years ago, my education into the culinary uses of mushrooms took off in earnest. Michelle is a sparkling personality, someone who in the crowded Saturday market, with her almost luminous enthusiasm and exuberant joy passing out samples of her cooking, I couldn't help but notice. What I found was that vegan cooking, which to me heretofore had meant flavorless food with more similarities to warmed up mattress fillings than real food – could, in Michelle's hands, be truly delicious. When Michelle and I talked, the topic soon turned to mushrooms, a topic which had begun to interest Michelle intensely beginning about the same time as that lightning bolt struck me.

Overcoming my dearly held dread of vegan food and encouraged by the wonderful flavor of her samples, we invited Michelle to our home to cook vegan meals for my family. At one of those dinners Michelle met Camille; the two of them found they had a mutual interest in developing a cookbook specially on mushrooms. Most currently available mushroom recipes feature heavy, fatty, rich sauces for use as toppings of meat entrées, but little is available for mushrooms as the main ingredient.

This book, put together by these two incredibly talented and motivated women, fills that niche, and the results are spectacular.

As you may have gathered, Camille is my daughter, our youngest. Camille trained at Savannah College of Art and Design in Industrial Design, she studied in Hong Kong, China, and elsewhere, where her extraordinary creativity has found a receptive audience worldwide. I have, of course, known Camille her whole life; I met her the moment she entered this world. She turned her head, looked directly into my eyes, or as it felt, directly into my soul — and I knew she was destined for great things. This book, I'm sure, is one of them.

So while the title of this book may be *Just Mushrooms*, a whole world of flavor, learning, and I hope, a whole new adventure exploring the culinary uses of these wonderfully fascinating fungi await you. It is a world in which what you eat improves your health while improving that of the planet. This is the food that awaits you on your new adventure.

My hope is that your journey through this book will bring you a broader appreciation for the world of fungi, but I can guarantee you one thing: try these recipes and you will be amazed, as I was, and continue to be, at the wonders wrought by *Just Mushrooms*.

Enjoy.
Mickey Myhre, M.D.

a nod to the power of passion

When we undertook this project, we did not know each other. We were brought together by a passion for mushrooms and a great desire to help others learn about all that mushrooms can do for us.

Our passion united us and we motivated each other to work. Creating during a pandemic certainly brought challenges. *Just Mushrooms* took on a life of its own as we continued to create through unprecedented times.

During the process of bringing *Just Mushrooms* to fruition we both lost close friends, unexpectedly and non-covid related. Both were young men, under 30, who believed strongly in a sustainable, plant-based, and a mushroom loving future – we offer this in their memories.

"When suddenly you find yourself alone after the death of someone you love, it can feel as if you are being given a new life and being asked what will you do with this life? And why do you wish to continue living." — *The Tibetan Book of Living and Dying* by Sogyal Rinpoche.

We answered the question of what we will do and why, with this, our combined passion project. We wish to help. We wish to show others the amazing power of mushrooms and create a more sustainable tomorrow.

In loving memory of Niko and Trevor we offer, *Just Mushrooms*.

about mushrooms

Mushrooms have a history in folklore and have remained mysterious to most. They have the potential to feed you, kill you, and heal you. Fungi make up one of life's six kingdoms (Archaebacteria, Eubacteria, Protista, Fungi, Plantae, Animalia), and are essential to life on Earth. We have fungi to thank for many of the foundations of life, as plants only made it out of the water around 500 million years ago thanks to their collaboration with fungi (Stamets et al. 2019). In the following pages, we hope to illustrate mushrooms' and fungi's crucial role in our world and how delicious their benefits can be.

Exploring this third kingdom, we are going to discuss the mushrooms and fungi used predominantly in this cookbook. All mushrooms belong to the kingdom of fungi, but their phylum, class, order, family and genus vary according to the mushroom type. When identifying mushrooms, looking at their method of spore dispersal can be helpful. This trait categorizes mushrooms into gills, pores or teeth.

There is a sense of poetry to mushrooms and fungi; they help create the soil we walk on, they serve as an underground communication network, decompose the dead, and their fruiting bodies serve as a source of nourishment. Part of the beauty of mushrooms is their mystery and abundance, even underfoot.

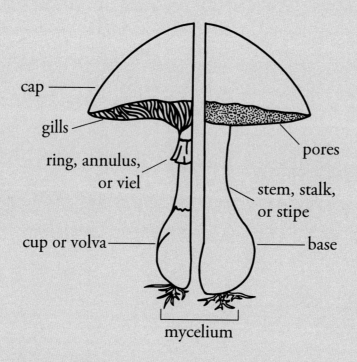

Mushrooms are the fruiting bodies of fungi, but for the most part they live underground, and are known as Mycorrhizal fungus (mycelium). Mycelium has a symbiotic relationship with virtually all trees and helps join trees together with an underground network affectionately called the "wood wide web" (Sheldrake 2021). Trees can communicate with one another and even recognize their kin by sharing carbon signals. Carbon is their universal language and flows through their shared mycelial network (Stamet et al. 2019). For this reason, mycelium is one of Earth's greatest carbon sequesters. Through plants, carbon is stored in their cell walls, then traded for nutrients with the mycorrhizal fungi. Once absorbed by fungi, it can be stored underground for thousands of years; even when the mycelium dies, the carbon remains locked underground, building a reserve for the future (Stamets et al. 2019). Over 70% of carbon actually ends up below ground through this exchange. The relationship between plants and fungi not only stores carbon for the future, but also indicates intentional design.

Mycelial intelligence is just starting to be unveiled, and both low-tech and high-tech biomimetic approaches are being used to reduce energy consumption and create less pollution. Mycoremediation is a hybrid of low-tech and high-tech approaches; this is the use of fungi to absorb, degrade, or sequester contaminants in soil or water. Fungi have been proven to absorb toxic oil spills, decompose plastics, sequester carbon and absorb heavy metals. Mycelium can also trap bacteria in contaminated drinking water, essentially acting as a micron filter. A low-tech application for this use is being studied by mycologist Trad Cotter, as a way to help impoverished communities filter their own water. A high-tech biomimetic application is the use of mycelium to grow packaging, leather, building materials, furniture and meat substitutes. When you look at the impact of our current meat consumption, the facts are startling. Livestock and their byproducts account for at least 32,000 million tons of carbon dioxide (CO_2) per year, which is 51% of all worldwide greenhouse gas emissions (Goodland and Anhang 2009). It makes sense to replace our current meat consumption with mushrooms, for both their sustainability and global health benefits.

Growing mushrooms requires few resources. They can be grown from cardboard, sawdust, straw, and other media with very little water and no light. Their life cycle is also very quick, as they can usually be harvested within a week. Mushrooms really seem to be part of the future of food when you look at their sustainability footprint and health benefits in comparison to our current agricultural practices. They can also be grown at home, making the connection to your food even more profound. Mushrooms have the unique ability to feed your mind, body and spirit in a way that's unparalleled.

We hope you enjoy exploring the kingdom of fungi in your kitchen and are able to master these recipes with a smile.

how to use this book

Before you dive into the recipes, I recommend that you peruse the sections detailing the mushrooms we've used. There are somewhere between 2.2 million and 3.8 million species of fungi on Earth. A mere 8% of all fungal species have been catalogued. We are just scratching the surface of what mushrooms can do. Those used in this book are considered to be fairly common and easy to acquire. They were selected for their taste, ease of sourcing, versatility for cooking, and health benefits.

The recipes created here are all original and lend themselves to substitutions, so don't despair if you can't find comb tooth mushrooms – use lion's mane instead. Can't find king trumpet mushrooms? Use black kings or a large cluster of blue oysters. In our sushi recipe we mention the Japanese art of wabi-sabi. Wabi-sabi is a worldview centered on the acceptance of transience and imperfection. This is especially poignant when applied to food, since our creations are quickly consumed and therefore transient in nature. This aesthetic is sometimes described as one of appreciating beauty that is "imperfect, impermanent, and incomplete" in nature. This is a good approach for working with mushrooms and not just when making sushi. You are cooking with powerful medicine and whether it turns out perfect should not be the focus – getting these delicious, amazing mushrooms into your body should be!

I'm often asked "how to encourage kids to eat mushrooms?" There are a few strategies I use with my own mycophobia-suffering tweens. I often hide the mushrooms. In the recipes for patties (like "crabby" patties or thai curry patties), the mushrooms are shredded and unrecognizable as mushrooms. Dried mushroom powders are another great way to hide them, like in the recipes for fairy rings or chowder. The lion's mane pudding is another easy way to coax kids into eating more mushrooms, because it is a dessert they will never know this rich cacao pudding is hiding a super powerful brain protector! We now know disease begins in childhood and develops slowly over time until it manifests as an autoimmune disorder, heart disease or cancer ("Heart Disease Starts in Childhood | NutritionFacts.Org" n.d.). There's never been a better time to get your kids involved in learning about food and its ability to keep them well or make them sick. Education is the other strategy I use with mycophobia-leaning youth or adults. Use this book as a springboard to get your family involved in learning more about the amazing world of fungi!

As you learn more about fungi here are a few practical considerations. Purchase mushrooms that are firm with a fresh, smooth appearance. Their surface should be dry but not dried out. Don't buy wet or smelly mushrooms. Once purchased, keep them in your refrigerator in a porous paper bag. Most mushrooms, if they were in good shape when purchased, will last a week in your refrigerator. If you purchase dried mushrooms or dehydrate your own, the best way to store them is in a glass jar with a silica pack (to absorb any moisture) in a dark, cool space out of direct sun.

Another practical consideration is the cooking of mushrooms for consumption. We sometimes find people tempted to serve or eat raw mushrooms. This is not the best idea as mushroom cell walls are difficult for humans to digest. Many species of mushrooms contain hydrazine, which has been found to make some people sick. To stay on the safe side, simply cook your mushrooms thoroughly. The cooking process helps break down fungal cell walls, rendering the mushroom flesh more readily digestible, but also releasing the significant nutritional value contained within the cells. Not to mention, the delectable flavors of our beloved mushrooms are released when cooking!

If you're working with dehydrated mushrooms, rehydration is fairly simple. Put the dehydrated mushrooms in tepid water and allow to reconstitute for 15 minutes (longer if your specimens are very thick). Use a tall jar, so any debris that may have dried on the mushroom will fall to the bottom of the jar while the mushroom will float to the top for ease of separation. If reconstituting in a broth, simmer on low heat until mushrooms are plump and full.

Finally, what is the best way to source mushrooms? Since mushrooms absorb everything it is important to be careful when sourcing them. Mushrooms grown in soil that has heavy metals, pesticides and other toxins will absorb these chemicals and then pass them on to you. The best source is usually your local farmers market. Do a quick internet search to see who is growing mushrooms in your area and where they sell them. Your local co-op or natural grocery store usually carries reliably sourced mushrooms. Be wary of frozen mushrooms, as their origin can be difficult to determine. Mushrooms grown indoors offer the cleanest, pesticide-free possibilities. Become friends with your farmer and/or forager and get to know exactly where your mushrooms came from. Foraged mushrooms, like morels, can also be found at farmers markets or directly through local foragers. Contact your local mycological association for help finding contacts from whom to purchase foraged mushrooms.

If you sit down to eat the Thai Curry Patties, which feature a mushroom patty on a bed of salad, are you more closely related to the lettuce or the mushroom? New research shows that the kingdom of fungi is more closely related to humans than plants. The genetic composition of mushrooms is similar to our own. They can help us get well, stay well, and live longer by healing us and our planet. Use them, grow them, and eat them! — *Michelle*

BREAKFAST

avocado toast

SERVES 2

Why pay someone else to make your toast? There are a million ways to do this and they're all delicious. We used a millet bread to give some heft to our toast offering. You can use any kind of bread and any variety of mushroom you fancy. — *Michelle*

---

1 tablespoon sesame oil

5 cloves garlic, minced

1 cup of chestnut mushrooms

2 tablespoons soy sauce

1 teaspoon maple syrup

beet sprouts, for garnish

1 large ripe avocado

bread of choice

For health benefits, see page 76

Fun fact: Avocado Toast is the #1 breakfast trend in the United States, with its popularity increasing nearly 50% and some 533,000 posts of toast being made this year. ("Avocado Toast Is a Top Breakfast Trend of 2017" 2017)

1. In a small saucepan, heat sesame oil and toast garlic on medium heat for roughly 2 minutes.

2. Prepare your mushrooms by removing the rough mycelial bottom and placing the stalks and caps in the pan.

3. Allow mushrooms to sweat and cook in their own garlicky goodness for 2 minutes.

4. Add soy sauce and syrup.

5. Cook another 2 minutes while you toast your bread of choice.

6. Place mashed or sliced avocado on toast.

7. Top with mushrooms and garnish with fresh sprouts.

pumpkin fairy rings

12 BAKED DONUTS OR 6 MUFFINS

In bygone times, people believed that fairy rings grew in the spots where fairies had danced. These deliciously moist, nutty pumpkin rings are sure to make you dance for joy over all the flavor they offer. You won't believe how moist these gluten-free, donut-like rings are. These also work great using a muffin pan. — *Michelle*

DONUT

2 cups Bob's Red Mill gluten-free baking flour

1 cup almond flour

2 tablespoons ground walnuts (use a coffee grinder)

2 tablespoons ground fairy ring mushrooms

1 cup brown sugar

1 tablespoon ground flax seed

4 teaspoons baking powder

1 teaspoon salt

2 teaspoons cinnamon

1 teaspoon nutmeg

½ teaspoon clove

1 15 ounce can of unsweetened pumpkin

⅔ cup coconut oil, melted

2 tablespoons maple syrup

FROSTING

1 ½ cups cashews soaked overnight (or boiled 10 minutes)

⅓ cup maple syrup

2 tablespoons brown sugar

2 teaspoons vanilla extract

1 teaspoon cinnamon

½ teaspoon nutmeg

¼ teaspoon clove

DONUT

1. Preheat the oven to 375 degrees.

2. Mix dry ingredients and wet ingredients separately.

3. Combine wet and dry ingredients, mixing until fully combined.

4. Fill the donut pan to the rim; if using muffin pan, fill ¾ of the way to the top.

5. Wet the back of a spoon to flatten the dough for donuts. For muffins, use the back of a wet spoon to shape the dough into a pointed muffin-like shape.

6. Bake for 15 minutes, for both donuts or muffins.

7. Use a butter knife to loosen the sides and flip over onto a wire rack for cooling. Don't leave them in the pan or they'll get soggy.

FROSTING

1. Drain water from cashews.

2. Put the cashews and other ingredients in a high-speed blender and blend until you get a decadent creamy frosting.

3. Allow your donuts to fully cool before frosting. Top with maitake "bacon" for the full experience (*see page 53 for recipe*).

*For health benefits, see page 76

savory morel corn waffles

SERVES 4

I adore waffles! These are extra fun with their infusion of smoky dried morels. The corn, onion and pepper play delightfully with the morels to create a super savory base for another of our mushroom dishes (*we recommend crabby patties page 28 or steaks page 39*) or as a stand-alone. They're also great for breakfast with a mushroom tofu scramble and some pico de gallo. — *Michelle*

---

1 ¼ cups non-dairy milk

¼ cup coconut oil, melted

2 tablespoons maple syrup

1 teaspoon apple cider vinegar

1 tablespoon ground flax seed

3 tablespoons warm water

1 cup cornmeal

1 cup gluten-free flour blend

1 ½ tablespoons baking powder

⅛ teaspoon salt

½ cup corn kernels

2 tablespoons chopped green onion

1 small red pepper, diced

2 tablespoons of dried morels, ground

*For health benefits, see page 76

1. Preheat waffle iron.

2. Use a coffee grinder to grind morels into fine powder.

3. Add 1 tablespoon of flax to 3 tablespoons of water and set aside.

4. Mix your wet ingredients in a small bowl. Place dry ingredients in a separate small bowl and mix. Combine mixtures.

5. Fold in corn, green onion, red pepper, and morels.

6. Grease waffle iron (if you need to).

7. Fill waffle iron and cook until crispy and golden brown.

ENTRÉES

"chicken" salad

Who doesn't love a nourishing, high protein lunch on the go? This super versatile "chicken" can be added to a bed of greens, used as a sandwich filling or eaten on its own. This is one of those dishes that I pre-make and eat all week. — *Michelle*

---

1 pound black king mushrooms

2 tablespoons olive oil

½ medium white onion, diced

2 cloves of garlic, minced

3 tablespoons poultry seasoning

1 15 ounce can of chickpeas

1 red bell pepper, diced

3 stalks celery, diced

½ medium red onion, diced

½ cup sliced almonds

½ cup dried cranberries

¾ cup vegan cream cheese

salt and pepper, to taste

OPTIONAL ADD-INS

halved red grapes

diced green apples

seasonal berries

For health benefits, see page 76

1. Use a sturdy metal fork to shred mushrooms. Place the mushroom against a cutting board and use the fork to pull the mushroom apart. Shred the cap and stalk of the mushroom.

2. Add oil to cast iron skillet

3. Sauté the white onion and garlic over medium heat until golden and aromatic.

4. Add the mushroom shreds and allow the mushrooms to begin to sweat.

5. Add the poultry seasoning and mix well.

6. Cook mushrooms for 10 minutes over low heat, then set aside to cool to room temperature.

7. Drain the chickpeas and then smash them into a paste (into a near paste, leaving a few chickpeas partially smashed and a few whole).

8. Dice the bell pepper, celery, and red onion (rough chop apples and grapes if using).

9. Combine mushroom "chicken" with mashed chickpeas, bell pepper, celery, red onion, dried cranberries and almonds in a large mixing bowl.

10. Stir in ¾ cup of vegan cream cheese and salt and pepper to taste.

"chicken" tacos

SERVES 4

When I first discovered black kings shredability I made everything I could think of: chicken pot pies, chicken enchiladas, chicken dumplings and chicken tacos. Tacos are a staple dish in our house. We sometimes prepare them with corn tortillas from the store and we sometimes make our own from heritage blue corn. Tacos are so versatile and can be topped with virtually anything. Use this "chicken" recipe as a base and let your imagination go wild to create a bounty of fun toppings. — *Michelle*

---

1 pound black kings

2 tablespoons taco seasoning

3 cloves garlic, minced

1 small white onion, sliced

2-4 green peppers (Anaheim peppers preferred)

OPTIONAL TOPPINGS

beans

cheese

cilantro, etc.

For health benefits, see page 76

1. Using a fork shred the mushrooms from stalk to cap into chicken-like strands.

2. Mince garlic.

3. Slice onion into long thin strips.

4. Sauté garlic and onion, until golden and aromatic over medium heat.

5. Slice green peppers into long thin strips.

6. Sauté peppers over medium heat and allow to start browning.

7. Add shredded mushrooms, and taco seasoning.

8. Add your favorite chili verde sauce or make your own.

9. Add your favorite toppings, beans and cheese for delicious, healthy tacos.

"crab" patties

SERVES 4

"Crab" Patties were my first mushroom creation for this book. The capers and artichoke bring out the crab taste while the shredded mushrooms provide the texture. These are especially fun accompanied by corn waffle (*page 20*) and the gravy (*page 56*). — *Michelle*

PATTIES

1 cup of cooked potato (boiled, mashed, and cooled)

½ pound oyster mushrooms

½ cup artichoke heart, brine reserved

2 tablespoons olive oil (for cooking mushrooms)

1 small white onion, diced

3 cloves garlic, diced

¼ cup of capers, brine reserved

1 teaspoon salt, or none (taste prior to adding salt)

1 teaspoon pepper, to taste

1 tablespoon Old Bay seasoning

OPTIONAL

add a quarter cup of fine diced jalapeño to potato mash for heat

BREADING

2 cups gluten-free panko bread crumbs

⅔ cup hemp hearts

⅓ cup nutritional yeast

¼ cup grapeseed (for frying finished patties)

For health benefits, see page 76

1. Preheat the oven to 350 degrees.

2. Boil potatoes and mash roughly, set aside to cool.

3. Shred oyster mushrooms and artichoke heart (reserving brine), using a food processor if available, transfer to a bowl. Final product should be a loose shred.

4. Add 2 tablespoons olive oil to a large pan, sauté onion and garlic over medium heat until fragrant and translucent, roughly 3 minutes.

5. Transfer sautéed onion and garlic to bowl with mushrooms and artichoke heart mixture.

6. Add capers (with 1 tablespoon of brine) to the mixing bowl, along with 1 tablespoon of artichoke brine.

7. Add potato mash (break up any large pieces), nutritional yeast, salt (if using), pepper and Old Bay seasoning to mushroom mixture. Add diced jalapeño, if using.

8. In a separate shallow dish, prepare breading: combine panko and hemp mixture.

9. Using your hands, mix until you can create a palm-sized patty (no thicker than 1.5″).

10. Lay out each patty on a piece of parchment paper or other nonstick surface.

CONTINUED

11. Roll each patty in the panko and hemp mix, coating it evenly – set aside.

12. Line a baking sheet with parchment paper, place patties on the baking sheet, and bake for 10 minutes.

13. Flip patties after 10 minutes, cooking for a total of 20 minutes.

14. Add ¼ cup grapeseed oil to a cast iron skillet, over medium heat.

15. Remove patties from the oven and add to the hot skillet.

16. Fry each patty, on each side, for about 3 minutes, or until golden brown.

17. Serve hot with your favorite vegan tartar sauce. Our favorite way to serve is on top of a cornmeal waffle (*page 20*).

lion's mane chowder

SERVES 4

When you are deeply connected to the creation of food, you also, by default, become deeply connected to the seasons. I look forward to each new season and the flavors, textures and delights it brings. This recipe was born amongst the rustling of golden leaves, shortening days, and longings for a cozy pair of socks, a strategically placed chair, and a good book. Prepare to be nurtured with the epitome of cozy creaminess. — *Michelle*

CHOWDER

6-8 red potatoes

1 large white onion, diced

3 cloves of garlic, minced

1 cup of cashews (soaked for at least 2 hours)

1 tablespoon of olive oil

½ cup nutritional yeast

½ cup dried lion's mane powder

1 vegetable bouillon cube

1 teaspoon dried oregano

4 cups of soy or other unsweetened plant milk

1 cup of filtered water

1 teaspoon pepper

½ teaspoon salt

TOPPING

1 tablespoon olive oil

1 small yellow onion, minced

1 clove garlic, minced

¼ cup of celery, chopped

½ cup fresh lion's mane pieces

splash of liquid smoke (up to a tablespoon, to taste)

For health benefits, see page 76

If you don't remember to soak the cashews ahead of time, you can heat them with your soup and then blend all together.

1. Scrub red potatoes, leaving the skin on and cut into bite-size wedge pieces.

2. Boil potatoes in a small saucepan until fork tender, but firm enough to be picked up with the fork, not mashed.

3. Rinse in cold water and set aside.

4. Mince garlic and dice onion.

5. Add olive oil to skillet over medium heat. Sauté white onion and garlic and brown until golden and aromatic.

6. Transfer sautéed onion and garlic to a high-speed blender. Add cashews, nutritional yeast, lion's mane powder, bouillon cube, oregano, and plant milk.

7. Blend on high until smooth and creamy.

8. Pour mixture into a saucepan and heat over medium low heat.

9. Add 1 cup of water, mix thoroughly.

10. Get topping ingredients ready, by hand tearing lion's mane into small thumbnail sized pieces. Chop celery, onion and garlic.

CONTINUED

OPTIONAL

serve with a dollop of plant-based sour cream or herbed vegan cream cheese and leek microgreens

11. Heat a skillet to medium high heat with 1 tablespoon of olive oil.

12. Add onion, garlic and celery, allowing them to begin to release their aroma and brown slightly, roughly 2 minutes.

13. Add lion's mane pieces and a splash of liquid smoke. Allow them to brown, roughly 3 minutes.

14. Add red potatoes to your creamy soup base.

15. Serve chowder in a heavy, earthenware bowl for the ultimate comfort effect, or if you're so inclined, opt for a bread bowl.

16. Garnish soup with topping mixture.

uramaki comb tooth sushi

MAKES 9 ROLLS

Sushi is an art and there are endless possibilities with this form. It yields itself beautifully to the use of comb tooth mushrooms for its seafood like smell and texture. This recipe features an Uramaki roll, which traditionally has the rice on the outside.

Sushi has a rich history and as you become more comfortable with the form, continue to experiment. While you're building your comfort level, be guided by the Japanese art of Wabi Sabi. "Both life and art are beautiful not because they are perfect and eternal, but because they are imperfect and fleeting." With sushi rolling, we want to encourage the celebration of this art form. Have fun and don't worry if you end up eating your first attempt with a fork – it will still taste wonderful! — *Michelle*

SUSHI RICE

3 cups sushi rice

3 ½ cups water

½ cup seasoned rice vinegar

2 tablespoons sugar

2 teaspoons salt

Pre-made sushi rice can be purchased from restaurants or made easily following these steps. It's also useful to have a sharp knife (for cutting the rolls), a small bowl of water (for wiping your knife clean), and a dish towel (for drying the knife between cuts). A good sticky sushi rice is the first step in creating high quality, beautiful, tasty sushi. If cooking your rice from scratch, follow the recipe below. Otherwise, skip to preparing your vegetables.

1. Wash the uncooked rice with running water until there is no more milky starch. Drain the rice and add to your rice cooker. Add 3 ½ cups of water and cook rice. Allow rice to sit when finished then gently transfer rice using a wooden spoon to a large mixing bowl (ceramic or wooden bowls work best). Place rice vinegar, sugar and salt in a small saucepan and heat to dissolve sugar. Pour vinegar mixture over rice and fold in with your wooden spoon. Allow rice to cool to room temperature before working with it further. Don't try to cheat and put the rice in the refrigerator or this will ruin your consistency.

2. While waiting for your rice to cool, prepare your vegetables.

3. Shred comb tooth or lion's mane mushrooms by hand tearing them into small pieces. Dry sauté these in a cast iron skillet with a little lemon, salt and pepper.

CONTINUED

SUSHI

9 sheets of nori (having 1-2 spares is a good idea)

1 lemon

salt and pepper, to taste

1 green onion, cut into thin strips

2 cups shredded mushrooms

1 avocado, sliced thinly

1 cucumber, cut into thin strips

5 spears of asparagus, cut into thin strips

2 tablespoons sesame seeds

2 tablespoons vegan mayo

1 teaspoon Sriracha (or more to taste)

2 tablespoons pickled ginger

2 tablespoons wasabi

2 tablespoons soy sauce

*For health benefits, see page 76

4. Mix 2 tablespoons of vegan mayo with 1 teaspoon of Sriracha (depending on desired spice preference, add additional Sriracha) and mix with shredded mushrooms. Cut green onion, cucumber, and asparagus into long thin strips. When cutting cucumber, it is best to make the strips from the firm parts of the cucumber and not use the seeds in the center, as they will add unwanted moisture to your finished rolls.

5. Cut avocado in half; place pitted half in the fridge for topping the rolls later. Slice remaining half for inside of your rolls, roughly 8 slices.

6. Lay your sushi mat horizontally oriented, facing you.

7. Place your nori smooth side down (if using a brand that is textured). Wet your fingers and add sticky rice, covering the nori while leaving a ¼" margin around the edges with about a 1" gap at the top without rice. The goal is to spread the rice thinly, roughly 2 grains in depth. Using 2 fingers, wet the gap of nori with water, just enough to seal it shut later and not enough to make it soggy.

8. To make Uramaki, flip the rice side of the nori sheet onto the sushi mat, keeping the gap at the top furthest from you.

9. Choose firm pieces of asparagus and place them in the center lengthwise across the nori. Add your cucumber strips, green onion, avocado and mushroom.

10. Start rolling by placing your thumbs underneath the bamboo mat and lifting the edge that is closest to you up and over the filling in the center. Use your fingers over the bamboo mat and gently press along the length of the roll. This action presses the rice and the filling together and prevents the roll from being too loose. Pull the edge of the bamboo toward you to fold it underneath your hands, then continue to roll the sushi away from you until you've rolled past the far edge of the nori sheet.

CONTINUED

TIPS FOR
SUCCESSFUL ROLLING

Cover your sushi mat with plastic wrap to avoid some of the sticking.

Place a small bowl of water for dipping your sharpest knife in by your workstation.

Clear an ample workstation space and have your prepared veggies laid out in an order that makes sense to you.

Enter this next step with the intention of creating art, practicing mindfulness and enjoying beautiful food.

11. Pick up your finished roll by squeezing the mat around it. Transfer to a cutting board.

12. Use your refrigerated avocado half, and thinly slice to adorn your roll. Sprinkle sesame seeds to finish.

13. Wet your knife and allow the water to run down the length of the blade for a smooth first incision. Cut the roll at the center and then half again. Repeat until you have 8 pieces.

14. Serve with your favorite sides: wasabi, pickled ginger, spicy mayo, and soy sauce.

oyster "steaks"

SERVES 4

Oyster "Steaks" were my first foray into cooking mushrooms beyond a basic sauté. I watched Derek Sanno's video and made his recipe the same day. This version includes my killer dry rub and home-made barbeque sauce. I discovered that varying the rub and marinade can create endless varieties, so keep experimenting. The execution of this recipe works best with two cast iron skillets, one for cooking and one for pressing. The dry rub recipe makes enough to keep in your spice cabinet in a mason jar. — *Michelle*

USE YOUR FAVORITE INGREDIENTS BELOW, OR USE OUR RECIPES FOR THIS METHOD

One large cluster of pearl oysters (roughly 1 ¼ pounds) *You can substitute blue oysters but as they are thicker, you'll need to cook longer.*

Olive oil

Marinade

Dry Rub

DRY RUB

1 tablespoon cumin

1 tablespoon paprika

1 teaspoon cacao

2 teaspoons onion powder

2 teaspoons garlic powder

1 teaspoon chili powder

½ teaspoon black pepper

½ teaspoon alder wood salt (if not available, use Himalayan salt)

¼ teaspoon lapsang souchong (if not available, use 1 teaspoon liquid smoke)

1. Start making your marinade if you're not using a store-bought version. Dice garlic and onions, add to a large mixing bowl.

2. Add tomato sauce, molasses, maple syrup, and balsamic vinegar to the mixing bowl with garlic and onions. Taste, and add pinches of salt and pepper to your preference.

3. In a separate medium bowl, start adding all the dry ingredients for your rub. Mix thoroughly with a fork.

4. Once you've prepared the marinade and dry rub, heat a cast iron skillet over medium high heat.

5. Remove the tough mycelial bottom from your oyster cluster, leaving them firmly in a cluster.

6. Add a tablespoon of olive oil.

7. Place the mushrooms in the preheated skillet and begin to brown, roughly 3 minutes on each side.

8. Once golden, sprinkle liberally with dry rub on the side facing up.

9. Flip mushroom so dry rub is facing down, sprinkle the top side with rub, and place the second cast iron skillet on top and begin to press.

CONTINUED

MARINADE

4 cloves diced garlic

1 small white onion, diced

1 12 ounce can tomato sauce

¼ cup molasses

⅛ cup maple syrup

¼ cup balsamic vinegar

pinch of salt and pepper

For health benefits, see page 76

10. Make sure there is enough weight to press the mushroom clusters down; either by hand with a dish towel, or use a weight (pot with water, or a brick).

11. If mushrooms seem to be getting too dry, add 1 tablespoon of oil to ensure there is no sticking.

12. Repeat this process approximately six times (adding a liberal sprinkle of dry rub with each flip) until mushrooms are flat, golden brown and aromatic. This whole process should take about 15 minutes total, depending on the size of your mushroom cluster.

13. The outer layer of your mushrooms should become crunchy with a layer of "gristle" on the outside.

14. Using your tongs, pick up the whole cluster and bathe the cluster liberally in your nearby marinade bowl.

15. Plate it on a cutting board to cut into individual serving sizes.

16. Add extra sauce or rub for garnish depending on your preference.

thai curry patties

SERVES 4-6

This is a spicy amalgam of flavors and colors to delight the palate and highlight a beautiful specimen of lion's mane. The patties combine yellow curry, sweet potato, spices and lion's mane to bring to life the flavors of the Indian subcontinent. The accompanying salad is a triumph of color and flavor. The spicy peanut sauce puts the entire dish over the top as a must serve. This is one of those dishes that people continue to talk about the uniqueness of, long after it was eaten. — *Michelle*

PATTY

½ pound lion's mane mushroom

1 medium sweet potato, boiled and mashed

3 cloves garlic, minced

1 large white onion, minced

1 15 ounce can chickpeas, rinsed and drained

3 tablespoons yellow curry powder

1 teaspoon salt

1 teaspoon pepper

1 cup gluten-free flour blend

1 teaspoon dried coriander

1 teaspoon cumin

1 teaspoon dried ginger

1 teaspoon paprika

3 tablespoons sesame oil (for frying)

SALAD

½ small head purple cabbage, thinly sliced

1 bundle asparagus, chopped into thirds

2 cloves garlic, minced

1 pinky finger-sized piece of ginger, minced

¼ cup gluten-free soy sauce

2 tablespoons sesame oil

1. Preheat oven to 350 degrees.

2. Hand shred lion's mane into small strips.

3. Peel and cube sweet potatoes. Boil until soft. Drain water and set aside.

4. Mince garlic and onion.

5. Mash chickpeas into a rough paste.

6. Roast peanuts with salt at 350 degrees for 15 minutes (set aside).

7. Combine lion's mane, sweet potatoes, garlic, onion, salt, pepper, and mashed chickpeas into a bowl.

8. Use your hands to mix and form into patties. Our patties are 4″ across and about 1″ thick, which allow for even cooking.

9. In a separate shallow dish, add 1 cup gluten-free flour blend, coriander, cumin, ginger and paprika.

10. Place formed patties in the shallow dish, and cover with seasoned flour blend.

11. Bake for 30 minutes at 350 degrees on a parchment lined baking sheet.

CONTINUED

SALAD TOPPING

3 carrots, shredded

1 green apple, cubed

½ of a cucumber, cubed

1 orange, cubed

1 large red bell pepper, sliced into strips

4 green onions, diced

handful of Thai basil, chopped

handful of mint, chopped

1 cup toasted peanuts, whole

SPICY PEANUT SAUCE

1 cup peanut butter

¼ cup Sambal Olek chili sauce

1 tablespoon soy sauce

1 tablespoon maple syrup

1 lime, juiced

(add up to 2 tablespoons of filtered water if sauce is too thick)

*For health benefits, see page 76

12. Slice cabbage into thin strips. Chop asparagus into thirds, discarding any hard parts at the bottom of the stalk. Mince onion and garlic. Heat a skillet with sesame oil over medium high heat. Sauté cabbage, asparagus with onion and garlic. As they begin to cook (3 minutes) add soy sauce and continue to stir fry until soft.

13. Shred carrots, using a cheese grater.

14. Cut green apple, cucumber and orange into bite-sized cubes.

15. Slice red bell pepper into long strips, dice green onion, chop basil and mint (reserving a few leaves for garnish).

16. Assemble salad: place cabbage and asparagus mixture at the bottom of the bowl or plate. Layer carrot, pepper, cucumber, apple, and orange on top. Sprinkle it with green onion, mint, basil, and peanuts.

17. In a small saucepan over medium heat, add peanut butter, gluten-free soy sauce, Sambal Olek chili sauce, maple syrup and lime juice. Stir until creamy, roughly 2 minutes.

18. Preheat a cast iron skillet with 3 tablespoons of sesame oil over medium high heat. When hot, add the patties and cook for 2 minutes per side.

19. Place toasted patty on top of salad and drizzle with peanut sauce.

20. Garnish with mint and basil leaves.

tinga tostada

SERVES 5

My mother, Gloria, used to entertain using this recipe to introduce all my friends to authentic Mexican cuisine. Every family has their own tinga recipe, but this is our family's take on a Mexican staple. Traditionally cooked with chicken and refried beans with epazote, this recipe lends itself to a quick and myco-friendly version. Any oyster mushroom variety, sliced thinly, will work for this recipe as well. One thing to note is that the sauce can be made and frozen to reuse, depending on how many mushrooms you'd like to cook. Feel free to adjust the amount of mushrooms for your needs and save the sauce for later! — Camille

---

2 ½ pounds of black king mushrooms

1 white onion, half sliced, half cubed

3 cloves of garlic, diced

1 bunch of cilantro, leaves chopped

2 tablespoons olive oil

2 tomatoes, chopped

1 7 ounce can of chile chipotle

black ground pepper, to taste

2 bay leaves

salt, to taste

1 15 ounce can refried black beans

1 package of tostadas

For health benefits, see page 76

1. Cut the base of the mushroom off if it is tough. With the cap of the mushroom facing away from you, shred the mushroom stalks using a fork to achieve the "shredded chicken" texture. Cut caps of mushrooms into thin strips.

2. Cut onion in half, slicing one half and cubing the other, set aside.

3. Dice garlic finely. Chop cilantro leaves and set aside.

4. Heat olive oil in a large skillet, add shredded mushrooms, ¼ sliced onion, and all of the garlic. Cook until the mushrooms are tender, roughly 4 minutes.

5. While the mushrooms are cooking, add the chopped tomato, ¼ sliced onions and 1 chipotle chile to the blender. Blend until consistency is a runny paste (similar to salsa).

6. Taste to add more chipotle for desired spiciness.

7. Add the blended paste into the large skillet with the oyster mushrooms, making sure to cover them.

8. Salt and pepper to taste, and add 2 bay leaves for aroma and flavor, simmering for an additional 3 minutes.

9. Heat the black beans on the stovetop, roughly 3-4 minutes.

10. Serve with refried beans smothered on the tostada, layer the shredded mushrooms on top of the beans, and top off the tostada with fresh cubed onions & cilantro.

white "fish" fillets

Leaning in to the fishy nature of the combs tooth helped inspire this recipe. Hand shredding helps you understand how to work with the texture of the mushroom. The little fuzzy ends create the flaky quality ascribed to white fish fillets while the stringy pieces weave together with the potato to make juicy bites. Can be made into fish sticks or fillets and served as classic fish and chips. — *Michelle*

½ pound combs tooth mushroom, hand shredded

1 cup cooked, cooled and mashed potato

5 cloves garlic, minced

1 small white onion, diced

½ cup nutritional yeast

½ teaspoon salt

½ teaspoon black pepper

2 ounces vegan mayo

2 cups gluten-free panko breadcrumbs

2 tablespoons olive oil

OPTIONAL

a tangy cashew cheese with dill and chives really heightens the flavor profile

For health benefits, see page 76

1. Preheat oven to 400 degrees.

2. Prepare mashed potato by chopping, boiling, draining and mashing. Make sure to have an even consistency since this will be your binding agent.

3. Shred the mushroom into small (roughly 1") thin strips using your hands. Place cooled mashed potato and shredded mushroom in a bowl to mix. Add minced garlic, onion, nutritional yeast, salt and pepper. Shape mixture into desired fillet size. Fillets should be moist and maintain their shape; if fillets do not bind, add more mashed potatoes. Do not make fillets more than 2-3" thick or they won't cook all the way through.

4. Use a basting brush to apply an even coating of mayo to fillet. Pour panko in a separate shallow dish. Brush fillets in mayonnaise and transfer to your panko dish. Use your hands to pack the panko around the fillet.

5. Transfer filets to a parchment paper-lined baking sheet and bake for 40 minutes, flipping sides at 20 minutes. While they are sweating, preheat a cast iron skillet over medium high heat with 2 tablespoons of olive oil to lightly fry the outside of the fillet to finish. Once in the hot frying pan, use the back of a spatula to press the fillets and encourage a little more moisture to cook out. Cook until golden brown (roughly 3 minutes), on each side. An air fryer is a great way to finish these without the oil. Simply set to fry for 10 minutes.

6. Serve with salt and vinegar chips, or fries for the classic "fish and chips" feel.

SIDES
+
SNACKS

ketch's shiitake popcorn seasoning

SERVES 4

In our family, we often indulge in fancy popcorn dinners and have competitions between the two of us. Ketch, my husband, was more methodical in his preparations and nailed down our all-time favorite recipe. This seasoning recipe makes enough for multiple popcorn feasts; store the seasoning in a mason jar and add it to your spice cabinet. Enjoy with your favorite movie or on an outdoor adventure. This popcorn tastes great, even cold. — *Camille*

16 dried shiitakes (4 ounces of mushrooms or 2 cups finely ground shiitake powder)

1 cup popcorn kernels

3 tablespoons pink sea salt

4 tablespoons garlic powder

2 teaspoons turmeric

1 teaspoon berbere (or chili powder)

½ tablespoon cayenne

2 cups nutritional yeast

3 tablespoons coconut oil

*For health benefits, see page 76

SEASONING

1. Place dehydrated shiitakes in your blender and blend until a fine powder consistency is achieved.

2. Add sea salt, garlic powder, turmeric, berbere, and cayenne to the blender.

3. Blend until everything is a homogenized powder.

4. Add nutritional yeast last and blend for roughly 4 seconds until everything is mixed.

5. Carefully remove the lid of the blender, making sure not to inhale this delicious spicy powder.

6. Transfer to a jar for all your future popcorn cravings.

POPCORN

1. Heat a tall pot over high heat, without any oil.

2. Add 1 cup of popcorn to the hot pot.

3. Stir without oil for roughly 3 minutes.

4. Add coconut oil to cover kernels.

5. Cover with lid and jostle the pot every minute.

CONTINUED

6. Cook popcorn until kernels' popping slows to almost a halt.

7. Once popping slows, remove from heat and allow stubborn kernels to pop for roughly 1 minute.

8. Transfer popcorn to a brown paper bag and add 5 tablespoons of popcorn seasoning.

9. Close the top of the paper bag and shake seasoning all over the popcorn inside.

10. Transfer to a bowl and enjoy!

11. Store any leftovers in a new brown paper bag, as this will keep the popcorn crunchiest.

maitake "bacon"

Many mushroom varieties can be transformed into a bacon-like topping. Maitake petals are my favorite for their crunch! They absorb all the flavor of your marinade and turn a crispy golden brown in the oven. They're an awesome addition to any recipe. — *Michelle*

7 ounces maitake feathers
1 tablespoon sesame oil
1 tablespoon maple syrup
1 teaspoon liquid smoke
½ teaspoon salt
dash of smoked paprika

This recipe serves as a great topping for Fairy Rings on page 19.

1. Preheat the oven to 350 degrees.

2. Separate maitake feathers (for "bacon" remove the top pinecone-looking pieces, commonly referred to as feathers, from the base).

3. Reserve base of maitake (can be frozen) for mushroom broth recipe on page 72.

4. Mix oil, syrup, liquid smoke, and salt in a small bowl and pour over maitake feathers.

5. Toss well and make sure they are evenly coated.

6. Bake for 20 minutes.

7. Use a spatula to flip the feathers to ensure even browning.

8. Return to the oven for 10 additional minutes.

9. Remove from the oven and dust with smoked paprika.

10. Allow your "bacon" to cool completely. It becomes crispier as it cools.

11. Add your "bacon" topping just before serving your dish as contact with anything moist will cause it to lose that bacon-like crispiness.

mexican "ceviche"

This dish is a refreshing and light fare. Comb tooth mushrooms have a naturally seafood-like flavor and lend themselves perfectly as a substitute for white fish. Serve with your favorite chips and load up on the health benefits of comb tooth! — *Camille*

---

1 pound comb tooth mushrooms

¾ cup lime juice

salt, to taste

3 serrano chiles or
    1 large jalapeño, diced

1 cup of cilantro, leaves chopped

½ teaspoon dried oregano,
    crushed

2 large tomatoes, chopped

½ small white onion, chopped

OPTIONAL

1 avocado cubed for garnish

crackers or tortilla chips

For health benefits, see page 76

1. Cut rough mycelial bottom off of comb tooth cluster.

2. Slice cluster into large cutlets, no thicker than 1".

3. Sear the cutlets over medium high heat in a dry pan to get a slight char on both sides.

4. Flip and repeat char until brown on both sides, roughly 3-4 minutes on medium to high heat.

5. Remove from heat, allowing to cool slightly. Place mushrooms on a cutting board.

6. Chop your mushrooms into cubes or bite-sized pieces.

7. Marinate the mushrooms in a glass bowl with the lime juice and salt.

8. Let it marinate in the refrigerator while you chop the rest of the vegetables.

9. Once you finish chopping vegetables, drain the juice from the glass bowl. Stir in the tomatoes, onions, cilantro and oregano.

10. Taste and add salt if needed. Marinate for a couple of hours in the refrigerator.

11. To serve, fill a small bowl and garnish with the avocados (if using), with a side of crackers or tortilla chips.

mushroom gravy

SERVES 4

My kids drink this like soup! Besides being a holiday staple, it's absolutely the best for biscuits and gravy! — *Michelle*

---

1 small white onion, diced

4 cloves garlic, diced

1 tablespoon vegan butter

4 cups filtered water

2 teaspoons dried sage

1 teaspoon oregano

1 ounce dried oyster mushrooms

⅓ cup cashews

¼ cup nutritional yeast

1 teaspoon salt (truffle salt, if available)

1 teaspoon black pepper

OPTIONAL

tapioca starch

For health benefits, see page 76

If your gravy is not thick enough, make a slurry using ⅓ cup gravy and 1 tablespoon of tapioca starch. To do this scoop out ⅓ cup of gravy and stir in the tapioca starch. When thoroughly dissolved add the slurry back into the stock pot and continue to stir over low heat until the gravy reaches your desired consistency.

1. Dice onion and garlic. Sauté in a stock pot over medium heat with butter until golden brown and aromatic.

2. Add water, sage, oregano, mushrooms, cashews and nutritional yeast. Simmer for 20 minutes.

3. Pour into a high-speed blender and process until completely smooth.

4. Return to the stock pan and allow gravy to slowly simmer on low heat for another 10 minutes. This will allow the gravy to thicken and the flavors to unite.

DESSERTS

5C – chaga cheesecake

SERVES 8, 8″ CHEESECAKE

I overheard someone talking about a conspiracy theory involving the 5G network and my brain wandered off to come up with the 5C. This is a cashew based cheesecake featuring five fun flavors: cookie crust, cherry, chocolate, chaga, coffee, and topped with a little extra chocolate and cherry for good measure. — *Michelle*

COOKIE CRUST

1 cup almonds

1 cup dates, pitted

1 teaspoon cinnamon

½ teaspoon nutmeg

½ teaspoon cloves

1 teaspoon coconut oil, melted

1 teaspoon maple syrup

CHERRY LAYER

1 ¼ cups raw cashews
  (soaked overnight)

¾ cup fresh or frozen cherries

⅓ cup melted coconut oil

½ cup agave syrup

½ cup coconut milk

1 teaspoon salt

1 teaspoon vanilla

CHOCOLATE LAYER

1 ¼ cups raw cashews
  (soaked overnight)

½ cup melted vegan chocolate

½ cup agave syrup

⅓ cup melted coconut oil

½ cup coconut milk

1 teaspoon salt

1 teaspoon vanilla

As you make each layer, place in the freezer for at least 20 minutes, allowing it to completely solidify, before topping with the next layer. Use a high speed blender to make each layer. Proceed this way until layers are complete. Allow to freeze overnight before topping. Defrost fully when ready to serve. If not assembling all in one day, drain the soaked cashews and store in a covered container in the refrigerator.

CRUST

1. For best results use a springform pan.

2. Use a food processor to create a chunky sand texture and then press into the bottom of an 8″ spring form pan. Press up the sides of the pan about a ½″.

ASSEMBLY

1. Place all ingredients in a high speed blender

2. Cashews should be soaked overnight at room temperature or boiled for 10 minutes prior to assembly.

3. Blend until smooth and creamy, making sure the cashews are completely smooth with no graininess.

4. Pour on top of the crust.

5. Repeat the process with the next flavor.

CONTINUED

CHAGA LAYER

1 ¼ cups raw cashews
(soaked overnight)

½ cup agave syrup

½ cup chaga tea

⅓ cup melted coconut oil

½ cup coconut milk

COFFEE LAYER

1 ¼ cup raw cashews
(soaked overnight)

½ cup agave syrup

6 tablespoons of your favorite
espresso or ¾ cup of strong
black coffee

⅓ cup melted coconut oil

½ cup coconut milk

*For health benefits, see page 76

TOPPING

1. Once fully frozen you can top your cheesecake.

2. Melt ¼ cup of vegan chocolate and allow chocolate to cool to room temperature.

3. Drizzle the chocolate on top and place a handful of cherries in the center.

4. Return to the freezer to serve later, or continue to defrost (roughly 30 minutes) and serve immediately.

lion's mane pudding

SERVES 4

The idea for this recipe came to me from tricks I've learned from a Japanese neighbor, Baba, in Tokyo. Baba was fond of playing tricks, like telling me to call her Baba and then letting me find out that it did not mean Grandma but was in fact a rude way to call someone an old lady! She let me holler this across our street with the neighbors staring at me while she laughed uproariously. Baba was a trickster with food as well. She hid vegetables in everything. When my son refused to eat something, she simply transformed it, so he didn't know he was eating it. This recipe is the same way – you won't know how good it is for you because it tastes so decadent! — *Michelle*

---

1 cup dates (pitted)

½ cup cacao

¼ cup powdered lion's mane
   mushrooms

1 avocado

1 tablespoon maple syrup

¼ cup organic coconut milk
   (add more milk if it's too thick)

OPTIONAL

Banana can be used in place of
or in addition to avocado

1 teaspoon of espresso powder
can be added for extra fun

For health benefits, see page 76

1. Blend all ingredients in a high-speed blender.

2. Serve in bowls with fresh fruit or eat alone.

lion's mane sugar cookies

This fluffy, nutty version of a sugar cookie is perfect for a lion's mane infusion. Enjoy them with or without frosting. We love them dunked in a hot beverage! — Michelle

½ cup vegan butter

⅔ cup organic coconut sugar

1 teaspoon vanilla extract

3 tablespoons aquafaba (chickpea brine – the liquid left behind in a can of cooked chickpeas)

¾ teaspoons baking powder

¼ teaspoon sea salt

1 ⅔ cups gluten-free flour blend

⅔ cup almond meal (not almond flour – the texture and flavor is different)

⅓ cup tapioca starch

2 tablespoons lion's mane powder

1 tablespoon unsweetened coconut milk

OPTIONAL

seasonal cookie cutters

1. Preheat the oven to 350 degrees and line two baking sheets with parchment paper. Set aside.

2. Soften vegan butter by allowing it to come to room temperature; don't microwave.

3. Add softened vegan butter to a large mixing bowl and beat until creamy.

4. Add sugar and mix on medium speed until fluffy and light, about 1 minute. Then add chickpea brine and vanilla, mix again.

5. Add baking powder and sea salt and blend or whisk to combine. Then add gluten-free flour blend, almond meal, tapioca starch and lion's mane powder. Mix on low until the ingredients are combined.

6. Add coconut milk and mix one more time.

7. The dough should be thick and heavy. If it's too sticky add another tablespoon of gluten-free blend and shape into a large ball.

8. Refrigerate for 30 minutes or overnight (dough can be prepared three days ahead of time).

9. Place dough between two sheets of parchment paper and roll to ¼″ thickness and cut into desired shape. Arrange on your cookie sheet, leaving about an inch between the cookies so they don't stick together.

10. Bake cookies for 10-12 minutes. Cookies should have golden edges and fluffy middles.

11. Allow to cool for 10 minutes before transferring to a wire rack. Cool on a wire rack completely before frosting (if frosting).

WELLNESS

chaga chai latte

CHAGA SERVES 24, CHAI SERVES 3

Looking forward to my morning tea is sometimes the only thing that gets me out of bed. It used to be black coffee and I suffered for years from coffee tummy and the anxious jitters. Adding chaga to coffee can diminish these effects, adding chaga to chai is my favorite. I love the deep flavors of homemade chai with the forest-like undertone of the chaga. — *Michelle*

CHAGA

4 ounces chaga mushrooms

6 quarts filtered water

CHAI

1 cup almond milk

2 ½ cups filtered water

5 whole cloves

4 cardamom pods

2 whole star anise

1 piece fresh orange peel,
    about a 4″ strip

1 large cinnamon stick

1 to 2 tablespoon maple syrup,
    to taste

½ to 1 teaspoon black pepper,
    to taste

¼ to ½ teaspoon ground ginger,
    to taste

2 tea bags of black tea

For health benefits, see page 76

Alternative uses for spent chaga include adding to mushroom broth on page 72.

CHAGA

1. Break a few 1″ pieces of chaga off. To break the chaga, place inside a pillowcase or box and use a flat-head screwdriver with a hammer to tap off pieces.

2. Take broken pieces and place in a large crockpot of filtered water.

3. Steep on low, keeping the temperature below 120 degrees.

4. Allow to steep overnight or for a minimum of 8 hours for a dark, rich, full bodied flavor of the forest.

5. Store tea in mason jars and reuse the pieces 3-4 more times, keep tea refrigerated. Store chaga chunks in an air-tight container in the refrigerator until next use.

6. Once the chaga is spent (the tea won't be as dark or as rich anymore) then dehydrate the pieces (*see dehydrating tips page 70*) and grind into a powder and continue to use (*see chaga cheesecake recipe page 60*).

CONTINUED

TIPS FOR DEHYDRATING CHAGA

Preheat oven to 110 degrees.

Place used 1″ chunks on baking sheet.

Bake for 8-10 hours.

Remove before any charring of chaga.

Set out to cool.

Once cool store in an airtight container.

CHAI

1. Combine milk and water in a medium saucepan over medium heat.

2. Add the cloves, cardamom pods, star anise, orange peel, cinnamon stick, maple syrup, black pepper and ginger.

3. Whisk everything together and bring to a slight boil. Lower the heat and cook at a gentle simmer for about 5 minutes.

4. Raise the heat and return to a boil. Immediately add the tea bags and remove from heat. Allow to steep for about 2-3 minutes.

5. Once steeped, strain using a cheesecloth and serve.

6. Now you have a crockpot full of chaga and a pot full of chai.

7. Take your favorite mug and fill halfway with chaga and half with chai.

8. Don't be afraid to play with your chai recipe; add more orange peel, try a dash of powdered lapsang souchong for a smoky taste or use fresh ginger for more zing!

lion's mane tea

SERVES 1

Purchasing mushroom infused teas can get expensive. Why not make your own? It's super easy and the possibilities are virtually limitless. Every time I have a little extra lion's mane I dehydrate it and save it for tea! Recommended teas used for this recipe are rooibos, hibiscus, matcha, and Earl Grey. Sweetened cacao also works nicely. — *Michelle*

---

1 cup filtered water

1 hibiscus tea bag
(excellent for blood pressure)

½ teaspoon lion's mane powder

For health benefits, see page 76

If you'd like to make a big batch of tea, the common ratio used is 8 ounces of dried mushroom to 1 gallon of filtered water.

1. Boil filtered water.

2. Add your tea bag of choice.

3. Allow to steep per directions on the tea bag (typically 4-6 minutes).

4. Stir in lion's mane powder.

5. Enjoy!

mushroom broth

SERVES 4

There is nothing more comforting than a steaming mug of savory broth to elevate your general sense of wellness. Mushroom broth offers endless health benefits and can be made and frozen in bulk. — *Michelle*

---

8 cups filtered water

½ ounce dried mushrooms (ours is mixed oyster variety, chestnuts, and shiitake)

1 medium white onion, diced

1 medium carrot, washed and chopped

2 stalks celery, washed and chopped

2 stalks of kale (tear leaves from stems)

1 small fennel bulb, cut into pieces with leaves

4 cloves garlic, chopped

1 finger-sized nub of turmeric, peeled

1 finger-sized nub of ginger, peeled

¼ cup soy sauce

2 tablespoons red miso paste

½ bunch parsley, stems included

2 teaspoons dried sage

6 large sundried tomatoes

1 tablespoon oregano

1 tablespoon cumin

½ teaspoon Lapsang Souchong (or ½ teaspoon liquid smoke)

1 teaspoon black pepper

1 teaspoon smoked alder wood salt (if not available Himalayan salt is fine)

1. Start with a large stock pot and bring 8 cups of filtered water to a boil.

2. Add dried mushrooms (equals roughly 1 pound of fresh mushrooms).

3. Reduce heat to medium low.

4. Allow mushrooms to reconstitute.

5. Add onion, carrot, celery, kale, fennel, garlic, turmeric and ginger.

6. Add soy sauce, miso, dried/fresh herbs (parsley, sage, sundried tomatoes, oregano, cumin, Lapsang Souchong), salt and pepper.

7. Simmer for 1 hour.

8. Strain the ingredients through a cheesecloth or large colander. Save spent vegetables for another batch of stock.

OPTIONAL

To make your broth even more healing, consider adding any of the following: black garlic, collagen-boosting peptide powder, dried medicinal mushrooms (lion's mane, chaga and reishi).

For health benefits, see page 76

turkey tail tea

SERVES 4

Turkey tail mushrooms have a delicious earthy flavor that combines perfectly with additions like cinnamon and other warming spices. These mushrooms were my first introduction to the world of medicinal mushrooms. My mother came down with West Nile virus in the summer of 2017. Thinking that there were no effective conventional remedies turkey tail tea was suggested. We introduced her to turkey tail tea in hopes it might help her immune system beat the virus. She immediately started showing signs of improvement; her headache, malaise and weakness were banished, and she has now integrated it into her everyday routine at home.

Many claim that this mushroom has to be steeped for 68 hours on low heat, but there are many ways to prepare it. Our crockpot method is simple, easy, and in our experience, effective. It's also delicious! — *Camille*

---

8 cups filtered water

2 cups dried turkey tail
   mushrooms

2 star anise

2 cinnamon sticks

*For health benefits, see page 76

1. Fill your crockpot with filtered water.

2. Place all your ingredients into the crockpot.

3. Set your crockpot to low heat and simmer for 48 hours.

4. Once your tea is ready, you can enjoy this throughout the day and reap the amazing health benefits of turkey tail tea.

5. Continue adding water to your mixture, along with spices if you choose, for another 2 cycles. We keep the crockpot on our counter and continually add to the tea throughout the week. Make sure to keep continuous heat.

6. These mushrooms can be used about 3 times until they need to be replaced with new turkey tails.

APPENDIX

health benefits

The world is unwell. Humans seem to have lost touch with themselves and their relationship to the planet. We are, as a species, sick. According to the World Health Organization, "An estimated 41 million people worldwide died of non-communicable disease (NCD) in 2016, equivalent to 71% of all deaths. Four NCDs caused most of those deaths: cardiovascular diseases (17.9 million deaths), cancer (9.0 million deaths), chronic respiratory diseases (3.8 million deaths), and diabetes (1.6 million deaths)." That means that 71% of deaths worldwide are caused largely by lifestyle choices ("WHO | World Health Statistics," n.d.).

We firmly believe that mushrooms are part of the solution to this health crisis and many of the other crisis points for our natural environment. In this section, you will find a brief description of the health benefits for the mushrooms we feature in this cookbook. Please keep in mind that this is just a quick reference and that a great deal more information on these and other mushrooms can be found by following our sources. Mushrooms provide some of the greatest hope for healing. Use this section as a starting point for your own research!

CHAGA *(Inonotus obliquus)*
Chaga can grow on a variety of different host species but is most commonly found thriving on birch trees in semi-arctic climates in the Northern Hemisphere. This fungus is not a fruiting body, but rather a sclerotium or mass of mycelium that is parasitic to birch trees. Chaga has anti-inflammatory, immuno-modulatory and hepatoprotective effects ("Chaga Mushroom | Memorial Sloan Kettering Cancer Center," n.d.). This mushroom is also an adaptogen, which means that it supports your adrenal system, helping combat stress hormones. And finally, chaga outnumbers most 'super foods' in its antioxidant concentration. It's 45 times higher than acai berries and an astounding 1,300 times higher than blueberries!

CHESTNUT *(Agrocybe aegerita)*
The chestnut mushroom is traditionally used in Chinese medicine for the well-being of the stomach, spleen and kidneys. The chestnut mushroom is particularly rich in copper and pantothenic acid (vitamin B5). The chestnut also contains folate, biotin, niacin (vitamin B3), selenium, potassium and riboflavin (vitamin B2) ("Agrocybe Aegerita – Also Known as the Chestnut Mushroom, Velvet Pioppino, Agrocybe Cylindracea, Yanagimatsutake, Zhuzhuang-Tiantougu" n.d.).

COMB TOOTH *(Hericium coralloides)*

Also referred to as Hericium americanum, lion's mane, coral tooth fungus, and bear's head tooth fungus. Comb tooth mushrooms are from the same family as lion's mane and possess many of the same healing properties. It is also a potent stimulator of NGF.

FAIRY RING *(Marasmius oreades)*

Fairy ring mushrooms grow in beautiful circles and are often found in grassy areas. Folklore maintains that these rings were made by fairies dancing in circles! Aside from their colorful history, fairy ring mushrooms are prized for their unusual, sweet taste. Sugar-like molecules in their fungal tissues protect the cells from damage when the mushroom is dehydrated, creating a sweet, nutty taste. These mushrooms are high in protein and fiber, while being very low in carbohydrates and fats.

LION'S MANE *(Hericium erinaceus)*

This medicinal mushroom is one of our favorites to cook with, most notably known for its distinct seafood-like qualities. Affectionately called "nature's nutrient for the neurons" by fungophiles, this mushroom has profound medicinal qualities benefiting our neurology. Lion's mane stimulates the production of nerve growth factor (NGF) and research has shown that increased doses of lion's mane can repair neurological trauma and slow down senility. Lion's mane also improves mental clarity and focus (Powell 2014).

MAITAKE *(Grifola frondosa)*

Maitake, also commonly called "hen of the woods" or "sheep's head," is one of the tastiest polypores, similar to eggplant in flavor. Usually found on stumps or the base of hardwood trees like oak, this mushroom is a favorite of foragers. Clinical studies have shown that high doses of maitake can be used to control blood sugar levels, as they have antidiabetic constituents. This mushroom is also highly regarded clinically in cancer therapy. Aside from cancer therapy and HIV therapy, maitake can be used to treat neuralgia, palsy, and various forms of arthritis (Robert Dale 2011). One wonderful attribute of maitake is that its vitamin D2 levels can be increased by sun exposure after harvesting. If exposed to 6-8 hours of sun after harvesting, vitamin D2 levels increase from 460 IU to 31,900 IU per hundred grams – that's nearly 70 times the vitamin D2 content! It's no wonder maitake is so highly prized for its culinary and medicinal benefits.

MOREL *(Morchella spp.)*

Morel mushrooms belong to the family *Morchellaceae* and should not be mistaken for the false morel. The true morel will be hollow inside from the tip of the cap to the stem. Speaking of which, they are delicious filled, breaded and fried. Morels are highly prized for their taste and have a long history of human consumption. Morels are high in potassium and help protect the heart. They have among the highest amounts of vitamin D of the edible mushrooms. Brand new studies show that morel mycelium extract can protect against liver damage from environmental toxins (Nitha, Fijesh, and Janardhanan 2013).

OYSTER *(Pleurotus ostreatus)*

There are many varieties of oyster mushrooms that vary in size and color. These varieties include pearl white, blue, pink, golden, phoenix and king. These commonly available mushrooms are a powerhouse of wellness for the mind and body. They've been used to develop antibiotics against some of our worst bacteria, like *salmonella* and staphylococcus ("A Review on oyster mushroom (Pleurotus Spp) | International Journal of Current Research" n.d.). Oyster mushrooms have the ability to lower cholesterol and triglycerides by an average of 40% in clinical trials. Oysters have also been shown to reduce markers of inflammation for diseases ranging from rheumatoid arthritis to irritable bowel syndrome. The high level of antioxidants found in oysters fights oxidative stress in many chronic conditions. Studies are ongoing, but oysters can also boost your brain health and fight cancer.

SHIITAKE *(Lentinula edodes)*

One of the more commonly sourced mushrooms, shiitake is equally delicious and nutritious. In Japan, it is known as the 'oak mushroom'; this is because shiitake's name is derived from its relationship with the shia tree, a Japanese evergreen oak. Shiitake is the second most commonly eaten mushroom in the world and has been cultivated in China since the Song Dynasty in 1100 AD (Robert Dale Rogers 2011). This mushroom has profound skin health benefits: taking 1500 mg of shiitake extract has been shown to improve acne (Tero Isokauppila and Hyman 2017). Cosmetically, shiitake extracts containing about 10% ergosterol are used for cell regeneration, wound healing and skin firming products (Robert Dale Rogers 2011). When extracted, shiitakes also contain the nutrient acetylated beta-glucan, which enhances the immune system. In Japan, more than 700 hospitals use this nutrient sourced from shiitakes as part of their protocols associated with chemotherapy (Robert Dale Rogers 2011).

TURKEY TAIL *(Trametes versicolor)*

Turkey tail mushrooms are a medicinal polypore (woody shelf-like mushroom) found throughout the world. These mushrooms have been used in Asia in traditional medicine for centuries. They possess a myriad of health benefits due to the polysaccharides they produce; polysaccharide K (PSK) and polysaccharide-peptide (PSP) have shown great potential as an adjuvant cancer therapy agent (Fisher and Li-Xi 2002). Specifically, studies have shown the efficacy of PSK as an immunotherapy or biological response modifier (BRM). BRMs have the potential to increase the ability for a host to defend itself from tumor progression. This mushroom has also been shown to enhance white blood cell activity and decrease inflammation. These benefits cannot be obtained solely from eating the mushroom, but instead are harnessed through slow brewing of teas or dual extraction methods.

about
michelle russell

I am a person driven by the constant evolution of self. I've been many things in my life: a mother, a teacher, a professor, a traveler, a yogi, a chef and a mushroom enthusiast. I like change and plunge headlong into new adventures, embracing new passions and evolving again.

I came to this moment in time, in Idaho, from a ten year loop. Ten years ago I changed everything about my life, lost 80lbs by adopting a plant-based diet, ridding myself of the need for 12 prescription medications, curing my depression, accepting a new job and moving to Tokyo. From Tokyo, I moved to Bavaria and spent years traveling the European capitals and backroads. During this period of exploration, I went to culinary school to learn more about the many ways that plants can heal us and became convinced that part of my next evolution of self would be to help make it easier to be healthy.

From this sincere desire, I started a plant-based company and began making fermented artisanal cashew cheeses. As a food producer, I became more aware of the gaps in the food supply and realized that cashews weren't sustainable. This launched me into a deep dive with mushrooms from which I hope to never emerge. Mushrooms are part of humanity's future survival. It is my sincere desire that this book's recipes launch you on your own deep dive into the wondrous world of fungi.

about
camille myhre degabrielle

I had the fortunate experience of growing up in a bicultural family whose love of food was the highlight of every day; my life was infused with a spectrum of cuisine and connection that left a lasting impression. My Mexican mother would always be filling the kitchen with spicy aromas, while my father enveloped the home with every genre of music. This lively upbringing gave me the advantage of perspective.

Idaho's outdoors also had a great impact on my life. Nature has always fueled my adventures and has been a well of inspiration. I always knew I wanted to focus on design opportunities that would give back to the landscape I've enjoyed.

I majored in Industrial Design at Savannah College of Art and Design, obtaining my BFA. During this time, I had the opportunity to study abroad in Hong Kong. Having a first-hand experience with manufacturing practices and seeing the impact of what product design could do to our environment, I refocused my efforts to more sustainable design. I then studied Sustainability & Biomimicry and allowed those principles to reshape my thinking.

When I looked at my own actions through the lens of sustainability, I realized I needed to make some changes. I adopted a plant-based diet for ecological and ethical reasons.

Knowing that I am making a difference every day for the planet and for my own health with every meal is something that I wanted to share with everyone. Mushrooms and fungi are tools to help us heal our bodies, our minds, and the planet itself.

My hope with this cookbook is that everyone can feel a greater sense of connection to their food and home, while enjoying a whole new kingdom of food!

acknowledgments

When you are on fire with the urgency of creation, you seldom slow down to be cognizant of the sacrifices the people around you are making so you CAN create. When we conceived this project together, we were not fully aware of the lengths we would go to in order to finish it! Waking at five in the morning became our new routine. Missed family dinners became standard. Asking our friends for endless help became our new normal. Not going out of town so we could work together became an acceptable consequence of our passion. This fury to work, to create this book, and these recipes, comes from the sincerest desire to help.

For our dearest photographer, Jeff, thank you. Thank you for seeing our vision. Thank you for your passion and professionalism. Thank you for continually striving for excellence. Thank you for bringing this project to fruition, whether that meant standing on a counter, carrying heavy slabs of granite, late nights, or eating mushrooms in everything. You were the man for the job! Thank you for believing.

To all of you who tried one of our samples, who shared a kind word, who sent a loving encouragement, thank you.

For everyone who buys this book, endless gratitude. Thank you for allowing us to be part of your journey with mushrooms. And thank you for being part of a narrative of pure intention to help, through inspired manifestation, and beautiful love.

FROM MICHELLE:

To Camille, my partner in writing, editing, testing, brainstorming, and passion: you made me believe. I am continually astounded by your professionalism and efficiency. Thank you for being my partner in this journey. The things we shared defy explanation. You have given so much to this creation, which allowed me to dig deep, rise up and match you. No one else would have undertaken a project like this, with a timeline like we created, and succeeded. The ease of this partnership is testimony to the pure intent behind this work. Thank you.

To my own partner, Spencer: you channeled some superhuman strength to carry the entire load of pubescent moody twins, a dying pet, eight surprise climate refugees from the Portland Fires (5 human, 3 animal), an unexpected return trip to Portland, a 115-year-old farmhouse in which I have a million unfinished projects, a full caseload at his own job, as well as my exhaustion and fear. His support, coaching and unwavering belief are why this book exists.

To my sons, Kevin and Kurtis: thank you for being feminists. Thank you for helping empower me and helping guide me through this world. Thank you for believing so strongly in me. Thank you for really seeing me and the intention behind my constant striving. Your help with the girls as they struggle to become independent speaks volumes to the men you are and their sacrifice during the writing of this book would have been far greater without your help.

To Ava and Grace: I am so proud of the way you've cooked your own dinners, done your own laundry, and are maturing into strong young women. I must seem so looney to your 14-year-old selves – up at all hours, endlessly muttering about recipes, pacing about, fawning over alien-looking mushrooms, and putting them in absolutely everything, much to your chagrin. I'm sorry! Thanks for being team players.

To the employees of The Kula Connection, LLC: Erin, Vince, Rachel and Chelsea, thank you for carrying this project on your backs by doing the work I wasn't doing! Thank you for putting up with my mutterings about mushrooms, having mushrooms everywhere, and being asked to recipe test endless mushroom dishes.

To Katherine, for your sweet cookies and moral support, thank you.

To Uncle Ta, Montgomery and Grace for their expertise with sushi, thank you!

FROM CAMILLE:

Michelle, I can truly say working with you has bettered me as a person. I always looked forward to our time together, and whether we were recipe testing, photographing, or writing together you always left me in a better mood and mindset than before. It's not often you find someone who mentors you in your creative endeavors and leaves you feeling recharged and filled with gratitude. You really do fill everyone with a little more joy and, of course, your delicious food! I'm forever thankful mushrooms brought us together for this book. Your curiosity and heart for the world of mushrooms is evident in the way you create and share your efforts. Thank you for sharing this journey with me and I look forward to our future endeavors!

To my husband, Ketch, I should have known that the morel tattooed on the bottom of your foot would lead me to magical places. You're constantly reminding me of what is important in life, and how to savor every moment. I appreciate the lessons in foraging and adventures you've included my family in on the hunt for mushrooms. I don't know many people who would encourage a passion project like this, during a pandemic, when everything is so uncertain. You're constantly reminding me to play and never subscribe to a standard life. Thank you for your support and encouragement throughout this chapter in our shared life.

To my Myco-Myhre family, I can't thank you enough for being my sounding board with ideas. I love that I have parents who want to trek through the woods for mushrooms, regardless of what the weather holds. We might not be the best foragers yet, but my time with you in the woods have given me all I could ask for. Dad, thank you for being my resource library and answering all my mycology questions throughout this process; your well of knowledge and curiosity seems endless. Mom, you helped with all of the little things that I would let slip through the cracks some days. Thank you for sitting through the editing process and ensuring this book becomes a success.

To my supportive girlfriends, it's amazing what we can all accomplish with each other's support. Sydney, thank you for recipe testing, offering your beautiful space, and always sharing our love of food. Diane, thank you for offering to recipe test and your honest feedback. Shannon and Claire, for your endless confirmations, suggestions, and time; you both have listened to me endlessly. To Pammie, for your keen eyes with editing, and suggestions, thank you. Juliana, thank you for sourcing mushrooms and for fueling this passion. And to Evan, who isn't a girlfriend, but rather a brother to me. You are the least-likely convert, but you tried every recipe with enthusiasm and kept Ketch company foraging when I couldn't. And Elizabeth, thank you for embracing mushrooms and diving into the myco realm head on.

index

bibliography

"A Review On Oyster Mushroom (Pleurotus Spp) | International Journal Of Current Research". 2020. *Journalcra.Com.* https://www.journalcra.com/article/review-oyster-mushroom-pleurotus-spp.

"Avocado Toast Is a Top Breakfast Trend of 2017." 2017. Well+Good. November 13, 2017. https://www.wellandgood.com/top-breakfast-trends-2017-avocado-toast/.

"Agrocybe Aegerita - Also Known as the Chestnut Mushroom, Velvet Pioppino, Agrocybe Cylindracea, Yanagimatsutake, Zhuzhuang-Tiantougu." n.d. www.Medicalmushrooms.Net. Accessed October 3, 2020. http://www.medicalmushrooms.net/agrocybe-aegerita/#:~:text=What%20are%20the%20nutrients%20in.

Birch Boys. 2017. "Chaga Mushroom: Benefits, History, Side-Effects, and Testimonials." Birch Boys, Inc. November 14, 2017. https://birchboys.com/blogs/about-our-chaga/5-reasons-you-should-be-drinking-chaga-tea.

"Chaga Mushroom | Memorial Sloan Kettering Cancer Center." n.d. www.Mskcc.Org. Accessed October 3, 2020. https://www.mskcc.org/cancer-care/integrative-medicine/herbs/chaga-mushroom.

"Chestnut Mushroom: 5 Top Health Benefits (Exciting New Data)." 2018. Urbol.Com. August 25, 2018. https://urbol.com/agrocybe-aegerita/.

Dr. Sapna Baghel. 2019. "Morel Mushroom Health Benefits and Side Effects- Foodthesis.Com." Research on Plants, Nutrition, Tea & Superfoods. July 2019. https://foodthesis.com/morel-mushroom-health-benefits-and-side-effects/.

Fisher, Monte, and Yang Li-Xi. 2002. Review of *Anticancer Effects and Mechanisms of Polysaccharide-K (PSK): Implications of Cancer Immunotherapy. Anticancer Research 22* (1737–54). https://www.researchgate.net/publication/11217840_Anticancer_effects_and_mechanisms_of_polysaccharide-K_PSK_Implications_of_cancer_immunotherapy/citation/download.

Founder, Dr. Edward Group. 2015. "Chaga Mushroom: The Immune-Boosting Superfood." Dr. Group's Healthy Living Articles. April 17, 2015. https://globalhealing.com/natural-health/chaga-mushroom-the-immune-boosting-superfood/.

Goodland, Robert, and Jeff Anhang. 2009. Review of *What If the Key Actors in Climate Change Are Cows, Pigs, and Chickens. World Watch*, November, 10–19. https://templatelab.com/livestock-and-climate-change/.

Guy, The Mushroom. 2020. "Marasmius Oreades: All About The Fairy Ring Champignon Mushroom." Medicinal Healing Mushrooms. February 27, 2020. https://healing-mushrooms.net/marasmius-oreades.

"Heart Disease Starts in Childhood | NutritionFacts.Org." n.d. Nutritionfacts.Org. Accessed October 14, 2020. https://nutritionfacts.org/video/heart-disease-starts-in-childhood/.

Jedinak, Andrej, Shailesh Dudhgaonkar, Qing-li Wu, James Simon, and Daniel Sliva. 2020. "Anti-Inflammatory Activity Of Edible Oyster Mushroom Is Mediated Through The Inhibition Of NF-Kb And AP-1 Signaling."

"Morel Mushrooms Benefits, Uses, Recipes, How to Hunt Them." n.d. Dr. Axe. Accessed October 6, 2020. https://draxe.com/nutrition/morel-mushrooms/.

"Mushroom Compound Suppresses Prostate Tumors." n.d. ScienceDaily. Accessed October 3, 2020. https://www.sciencedaily.com/releases/2011/05/110523091539.htm.

Nasiry, Davood, Ali Reza Khalatbary, and Mohammad Ali Ebrahimzadeh. 2017. "Anti-Inflammatory and Wound-Healing Potential of Golden Chanterelle Mushroom, Cantharellus Cibarius (Agaricomycetes)." *International Journal of Medicinal Mushrooms* 19 (10): 893–903. https://doi.org/10.1615/IntJMedMushrooms.2017024674.

Nitha, B., P. V. Fijesh, and K. K. Janardhanan. 2013. "Hepatoprotective Activity of Cultured Mycelium of Morel Mushroom, Morchella Esculenta." Experimental and Toxicologic Pathology: Official Journal of the Gesellschaft Fur Toxikologische Pathologie 65 (1–2): 105–112. https://doi.org/10.1016/j.etp.2011.06.007.

Powell, Martin. 2014. *Medicinal Mushrooms: A Clinical Guide.* Eastbourne, East Sussex, Uk: Mycology Press, An Imprint Of Bamboo Publishing Ltd.

Robert Dale Rogers. 2011. *The Fungal Pharmacy: The Complete Guide to Medicinal Mushrooms and Lichens of North America.* Berkeley, California: North Atlantic Books.

Sheldrake, Merlin. 2021. *ENTANGLED LIFE: How Fungi Make Our Worlds, Change Our Minds and Shape Our Futures.* S.L.: Vintage.

Shomali, Naznoosh, Okan Onar, Basar Karaca, Nergiz Demirtas, Arzu Coleri Cihan, Ilgaz Akata, and Ozlem Yildirim. 2019. "Antioxidant, Anticancer, Antimicrobial, and Antibiofilm Properties of the Culinary-Medicinal Fairy Ring Mushroom, Marasmius Oreades (Agaricomycetes)." *International Journal of Medicinal Mushrooms* 21 (6): 571–582. https://doi.org/10.1615/IntJMedMushrooms.2019030874.

Stamets, Paul, and C. Dusty Wu Yao. 2002. *MycoMedicinals An Informational Treatise on Mushrooms.* Olympia, WA: MycoMedia Productions, a division of Fungi Perfecti, LLC.

Stamets, Paul, Louie Schwartzberg, Michael Pollan, and Et Al. 2019. *Fantastic Fungi: How Mushrooms Can Heal, Shift Consciousness & Save the Planet.* San Rafael (California): Earth Aware.

Tero Isokauppila, and Mark H. Hyman. 2017. *Healing Mushrooms: A Practical and Culinary Guide to Using Mushrooms for Whole Body Health.* New York, New York: Avery, An Imprint Of Penguin Random House.

"Trametes Versicolor." 2020. Wikipedia. May 10, 2020. https://en.wikipedia.org/wiki/Trametes_versicolor.

Vlasenko, Vyacheslav, Dejidmaa Turmunkh, Enkhtuya Ochirbat, Dondov Budsuren, Kherlenchimeg Nyamsuren, Javkhlan Samiya, Burenbaatar Ganbaatar, and Anastasia Vlasenko. 2019. "Medicinal Potential of Extracts from the Chanterelle Mushroom, Cantharellus Cibarius (Review) and Prospects for Studying Its Strains from Differs Plant Communities of Ultracontinental Regions of the Asia." *BIO Web of Conferences* 16: 00039. https://doi.org/10.1051/bioconf/20191600039.

Made in the USA
Las Vegas, NV
28 November 2020